Advent Guide for Families:
time to indwell the story

created by Trevecca Okholm

This Advent Guide for Families is created by Trevecca Okholm (certified Christian Educator PC/USA/ professor of practical theology, Azusa Pacific University) with special thanks to Los Angeles artist John August Swanson and his artwork for Advent.

© 2016 John August Swanson | Eyekons

additional credits include: Children & Worship, Godly Play, Living the Christian Year, Gross (2009, IVP), Common Prayer, Claiborne, Wilson-Hartgrove, Okoro (2010, Zondervan, The Jesus Storybook Bible, Jones (2007, Zondervan), The Way to Bethlehem, Biffi (1997, Eerdmans), Google Images. Cover photo: Cradle-to-Cross wreath joywares.ca. Wooden figures: worshipwoodworks.com.

A note to parents...

Here we go again! Christmas is almost upon us. I am beginning to feel the constriction of angst in my soul as I—along with my children, my grandchildren and my culture—again engage the rush and consumerism that has come to define the celebration of Christmas in North America.

Would I be correct to assume that you, like I, have a love/fear relationship with the season that now stretches out to begin marketing these days even before Halloween and yet so busily neglects to include the W A I T I N G of Advent?

This is a simple little book and I hope an easy way to guide you *with* your family through the weeks of Advent W A I T I N G and remain with you a little while beyond Christmas to include bringing the gentle light of Epiphany into your home.

My hope for your family is that this book might *live* on your kitchen table along side your family Advent wreath during this season of W A I T I N G as a means of preparing your hearts and home for the Christ child.

Because it goes hand in hand with the Advent wreath and the sight and smells of burning candles perhaps it will be easy and inviting for your family this season.

This is my prayer for you and all who dwell below your roof.

If you have any ideas for how this book might be improved, I would love to have your input! You are welcome to contact me at: tokholm@apu.edu

With prayers for abundant and gentle peace.....

First Week of Advent

START HERE:
This is the season of Advent, the time we get ready to celebrate the mystery of Christmas, this is the time when we are *all* on our way to Bethlehem.

....

But who will show us the way? *(each week of Advent we will take our directions from the different people we meet along the journey)*

....

Traditionally, during the **first week of Advent** we remember the **prophets** who lived a long, long time ago and *listened to* God and *spoke God*'s *Word . . .* the prophets of old show us that the way to Bethlehem is by *listening*.

....

On this 1ˢᵗ Sunday of Advent light the 1ˢᵗ purple candle of your Advent wreath – then read aloud the responses and Scripture passages on the following page…

Nativity © 2016 John August Swanson | Eyekons

First Week of Advent - FAMILY call to SABBATH

Begin with a Family Call to Sabbath read by parent or other adult: *We light the candle of HOPE on this first week of Advent. The light from these candles, that grow brighter every week, remind us that.....*

Family response read together:

> *.... Jesus Christ is the light of the world!*

....

READ the Bible aloud (if you have younger children, you may wish to read the Old Testament & New Testament readings only—you may also want to read from *The Jesus Storybook Bible,* by Sally Lloyd-Jones, pg. 144-151)

Psalm: Psalm 27
Old Testament reading: Isaiah 9:1-7
New Testament reading: 1 John 1:6-7
Gospel reading: John 1:1-18

....

✦✦✦✦✦✦✦✦✦✦✦✦

First Week of Advent - Family Talk-about-it

Were you listening carefully? What did God ask Isaiah to do?*
Wow! That's an important job. What would it feel like for God to give your family an important job like God gave Isaiah?
Would you be afraid to bring that message to "get ready!" or would you be joyful? Why or why not?

What important job does God have for your family to do this Advent season? Are you ready? Can you make a list of ideas? Can you do it? Let's make a plan together.

*God asked Isaiah to tell people what was going to happen, try to get them to listen, and encourage them to get ready for the coming of Christ.

End your Family Sabbath with Prayer Time
(you may say your own and end with the Family Sabbath Prayer and Blessing below)

Dear Lord, as we prepare our hearts and our home for your coming this Christmas, help us to be part of your plan to let the whole world know your love and your hope for the world. **Amen.**

....

The tradition of lighting a new candle each week of Advent reminds Christians to live into the accumulating brightness and hope of Christ even as daylight diminishes and darkness rises with the approach of the winter solstice. (see: John 1)

....

Advent in the history of the church – DID YOU KNOW?

Did you know that it was during the 6th Century that Pope Gregory the Great established the beginning of an Advent season for the church by creating four special masses for the four Sundays leading up to Christmas Day?

Daily Family Readings for this first week of Advent

(you may want to relight your Advent candle each day of the week)

....

MONDAY of this week: Read Isaiah 9: 1-7 again and talk about the hope of *light*.

- What is light and why is it important? What light do you think Isaiah was talking about?

- Did you know that Isaiah lived 2000 years before Christ was born?! Look in a dictionary and find out what the word *prophet* means.

- Do you think there are any "prophets" living today who show us the way to listen to God? Can you name them?

- In what ways do you think learning the Bible & listening to God are like *walking in light?*

- What are some ways that our world lives in darkness?
PRAY together for our world today.

End your family talk with a Celtic blessing before you *hush** the 1ˢᵗ Advent Candle:
May the peace of the Lord Christ go with you, wherever He may send you. May He guide you through the wilderness, protect you through the storm. May He bring you home rejoicing at the wonders He has shown you. May He bring you home rejoicing once again into our doors. **hush is a meaningful way to name the act of putting out the candle flame.*

Daily Family Readings for this first week of Advent

(you may want to relight your Advent candle each day of the week)

....

TUESDAY of this week: Read Isaiah 8:18-22 and talk about how God wants us to be *signs & symbols* in the world.

- What do you think that means to be *signs & symbols*?

- Talk about ways your family might become a *sign & symbol* of hope in your neighborhood, then PRAY for your neighbors.

End your family talk with this blessing of St. Patrick before you *hush* **the Advent Candle:**
May the strength of God pilot us; may the wisdom of God instruct us; may the hand of God protect us; may the word of God direct us and be always ours this day and forever more. **Amen.**

....

WEDNESDAY of this week: Read John 1:1-18 and wonder together why God sent Jesus into our world.

- What do you know about John the Baptist? You might want to read his story, "Heaven Breaks Through," in *The Jesus Storybook Bible*, pg. 200-207

End your family talk with a Scottish blessing before you *hush* **the Advent Candle:**
If there is righteousness in the heart, there will be beauty in the character. If there is beauty in the character, there will be harmony in the home. If there is harmony in the home, there will be order in the nation. If there is order in the nation, there will be peace in the world. So let it be.

Daily Family Readings for this first week of Advent
(you may want to relight your Advent candle each day of the week)

....

THURSDAY of this week:

Read John 1:19-34 and wonder together about why John called Jesus *the lamb of God,* why God sent the Holy Spirit *like a dove,* and why John said that he was *not worthy to untie the straps of Jesus' sandals?*

PRAY together for wisdom and understanding.

End your family talk with this Swiss blessing (Edelweiss) **before you** *hush* **the Advent Candle:**

May the Lord, mighty God, bless, preserve you and keep you, give you peace, perfect peace, courage in every endeavor. Lift up your eyes and see His face, and His grace forever. May the Lord, mighty God, bless, preserve you and keep you!

....

FRIDAY of this week:
Read John 1: 35-50 and wonder together why the world often celebrates the birth of Jesus at Christmas but forgets Jesus' mission to *call and teach* in the world. PRAY this week for your family to slow down this Advent season and make intentional time to dwell in the mystery of God's love and God's plan and God's *hope* for the world.

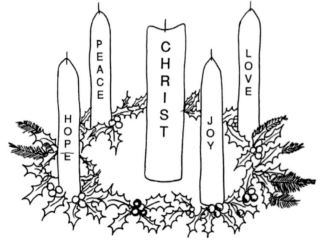

End your family talk with a blessing from Philippians 4:7 before you *hush* **the Advent Candle:**

May the peace of God, that transcends all human understanding, guard your hearts and your minds in Christ Jesus.

Second Week of Advent

During this *second* week of Advent we remember **the Holy Family**, who, against all odds, trusted the message from God and risked everything to be part of God's plan of salvation for the world . . . They show us the way to Bethlehem is by *trusting*.

....

DID YOU KNOW? The color of Advent is usually **purple** (or **blue**)? In ancient history the color purple often marked the coming of a king or Caesar. *(Did you know that in history, sometimes members of the royal family were the only people allowed to wear purple?)*

....

On this second Sunday of Advent light the 1st *and* the 2nd purple candle of your Advent wreath – then read aloud the responses and Scripture passages on the following page….

Flight into Egypt © 2016 John August Swanson | Eyekons

Second Week of Advent - FAMILY call to SABBATH

Begin with a Family Call to Sabbath read by parent or other adult:

Be present at our table, Lord. As we light these candles...

Family response: ....*we celebrate the peace coming into our hearts and our home.*

Parent or other adult: *Peace is like a light shinning in a dark place.*

....

READ aloud *(if you have younger children, you may wish to read only the Gospel reading. You may also want to read from* The Jesus Storybook Bible*, by Sally Lloyd-Jones, pg. 176-183*

Psalm: Psalm 122
Old Testament reading: Isaiah 11:1-10
New Testament reading: 2 Peter 3:8-15a
Gospel reading: Luke 1:26-33, 46-47

....

Family Prayer *Dear Lord, as we prepare our hearts and our home for your coming this Christmas, help us to be part of your plan to let the whole world know your peace, your love, your hope and your joy. Help us to trust you and be faithful.*

Second Week of Advent
Family Talk-about-it

- What would it feel like if an angel of the Lord suddenly appeared to one of us with an important announcement?
- Do you think that Mary was afraid? Why or why not?
- How did Joseph react when he heard?

A Visit © 2016 John August Swanson | Eyekons

- Could you trust God for such an important task?
- Is trusting always hard?

Wonder together about trusting God and having faith—especially at Christmas time.

....

End your Family Sabbath with Prayer Time *(you may say your own and end with the Family Sabbath Prayer and Blessing below)*

Blessing (before you *hush* your 1st & 2nd Advent candles)
May the light of Christ come into our home this Advent season. May the light of Christ lead us to the peace of God's Kingdom. Now and forever. **Amen.**

....

Advent in the history of the church – DID YOU KNOW?
Advent, means "the coming," it is a time of year when we wait *expectantly*. Like Mary, we celebrate the coming of the baby, Jesus—the Christ child. This year we wait in expectation for the full coming of God's reign on earth and for the return of Christ. And all Christians say, *Even so, come quickly Lord.*

Daily Family Readings for this second week of Advent
(you may want to relight your Advent candle each day of the week)

....

MONDAY of this week: Read Luke 1:26-33, 46-47 again *(optional in The Jesus Storybook Bible: pgs 170-175).*

- Why do you think the Scripture say that Mary was *favored?*
- Wonder together how hard it was for Mary to say what she did in Luke 1:38.
- Think of some ways that you might *trust* God more, *maybe make a list*

End your family talk with a Celtic blessing before you *hush* the Advent Candle:
May the peace of the Lord Christ go with you, wherever He may send you. May He guide you through the wilderness, protect you through the storm. May He bring you home rejoicing at the wonders He has shown you. May He bring you home rejoicing once again into our doors.

....

TUESDAY of this week: Read Psalm 122. *This is David's song of praise and prayer for Jerusalem.* This Psalm calls us to worship. It is one of the 15 *Songs of Ascent (Ps 120-134)* most likely sung by ancient Jews on their annual festival pilgrimages.
- Why do you think the people come together to worship?
- What do you think they expect to find?
This Psalm teaches us how to pray today for prosperity, peace and security.
Pray for our church family today and then end with this blessing:

End your family talk with this blessing of St. Patrick before you *hush* the Advent Candle: *May the strength of God pilot us; may the wisdom of God instruct us; May the hand of God protect us; may the word of God direct us; Be always ours this day and forever more. Amen.*

Daily Family Readings for this second week of Advent

(you may want to relight your Advent candle each day of the week)

....

WEDNESDAY of this week:

Read Isaiah 11:1-10. Use the images in this picture → as you read and talk about this passage from Isaiah.

- Picture a tiny vine sprouting out of a dead stump.

Even today the prayers of God's faithful people plant tiny seeds of hope and beauty in our world. Today, as you go to school or work or play….keep your eyes open and look for signs of faith and hope and beauty in your world.

PRAY together for trust, and hope, and beauty…and later today or tomorrow, *remember to tell one another where you saw signs of hope and beauty in your world.*

End your family talk with a Scottish blessing before you *hush* the Advent Candle:

If there is righteousness in the heart, there will be beauty in the character. If there is beauty in the character, there will be harmony in the home. If there is harmony in the home, there will be order in the nation. If there is order in the nation, there will be peace in the world. So let it be.

Daily Family Readings for this second week of Advent
(you may want to relight your Advent candle each day of the week)

....

THURSDAY of this week: Read 2 Peter 3:8-15a. Peter reminds us to be faithful and diligent. Talk about what "faithful" and "diligent" mean:
- How can your family encourage each other to be faithful and diligent in this world?
- What do you think you might want to do together this Advent season to remember how patient God has been with each one of His children?
- Does this change the way you *wait patiently* for Christ's coming this Christmas?

Pray together for patience and hope.

End your family talk with this Swiss blessing (Edelweiss) **before you *hush* the Advent Candle:** *May the Lord, mighty God, bless, preserve you and keep you. Give you peace, perfect peace, courage in every endeavor. Lift up your eyes and see His face, and His grace forever. May the Lord, mighty God, bless, preserve you and keep you!"*

....

FRIDAY of this week: Re-read John 1: 35-50 (from last week) and wonder together again why the world often celebrates the birth of Jesus at Christmas but forgets Jesus' mission to *call and teach.*

PRAY again this week for your family to slow down this Advent season and make intentional time to dwell in the mystery of God's plan for the world.

End your family talk with a blessing from Philippians 4:7 before you *hush* the Advent Candle: *May the peace of God, that transcends all human understanding, guard your hearts and your minds in Christ Jesus.*

Third Week of Advent

Shepherds are a rather dirty, smelly, bunch and they prefer hanging out with their sheep on quiet hillsides to being in the middle of town with all the people rushing to and fro. When you read the shepherd's story in Luke 2:8-20 (*The Jesus Storybook Bible, pg. 184-191*) just try to imagine how the shepherds felt when an angels appeared.

....

The beautiful gift of the shepherds is that they were the very first *missionaries!* After they saw the Christ child, the Bible tells us that they hurried out to tell everyone the good news!

The shepherds show us the way to Bethlehem by *coming to see and going out to tell!*

The Shepherds © 2016 John August Swanson | Eyekons

<u>Third Week of Advent</u> – FAMILY call to SABBATH

On this third Sunday of Advent light the 1ˢᵗ, 2ⁿᵈ, & 3ʳᵈ purple candle of your Advent wreath *(sometimes we use a PINK candle for this 3ʳᵈ week of Advent. Here's a challenge, see if you and your family can find out why!)*

....

A Family Call to Sabbath from a parent or other adult: *Be present at our table Lord. Joy is like a light shining in a dark place.*

Family response: *As we light this candle we celebrate the joy we find in Jesus Christ!*

....

READ aloud together: *(if you have younger children, you may wish to read only the Psalm and Gospel reading. You might also want to read from* <u>The Jesus Storybook Bible</u> *by Sally Lloyd-Jones, pg. 184-191)*

Psalm: Psalm 23
Old Testament reading: Isaiah 62:10-12
New Testament reading: Titus 3:4-7
Gospel reading: Luke 2:8-20

....

Third Week of Advent - Family Talk-about-It

- How would you like to be a shepherd?
- Wonder if it would be hard work?
- Do you think you would be lonely?
- Why is a shepherd's job important?
- Do you think that the shepherds were afraid when a bunch of angels showed up? Why?
- I wonder what the shepherds talked about on their way to Bethlehem?

Read Luke 2:20 again and talk about what the shepherds did after they saw baby Jesus?

Close with a family prayer time—you may say your own and end with the Family Sabbath Prayer and Blessing below….

....

End your Family Sabbath with Prayer Time *(you may say your own and end with the Family Sabbath Prayer and Blessing below)*
Dear Lord, as we prepare our hearts and our home for your coming this Christmas, help us to be part of your plan to let the whole world know your hope, your peace, your joy and your love. **Amen.**

....

Blessing (before you *hush* your 1ˢᵗ, 2ⁿᵈ, & 3ʳᵈ Advent candles)

May the light of Christ come into our home this Advent season. May the light of Christ lead us to the joy of His Kingdom. Now and forever. **Amen.**

....

Advent in the history of the church – DID YOU KNOW?
By lighting a new candle each week, Christian homes throughout the history of the church have added to the growing brightness. We sanctify our home in the coming light of Christ in a very tangible way—even as daylight diminishes and darkness rises with the approach of the winter solstice. Lighting the Advent wreath in our homes and churches enacts our faith in St. John's testimony: "The light shines in the darkness, and the darkness did not overcome it." – John 1:5

Daily Family Readings for this third week of Advent

(you may want to relight your Advent candle each day of the week)

....

MONDAY of this week: Read Psalm 23 again.
- What is your favorite part of this story?
- Why do you think that this is a favorite Psalm for so many people?
- How do you think "the rod and the staff" comfort the sheep?
- What does God use to comfort you?
- In verse 6, wonder together what it feels like to "dwell in the house of the Lord" for your whole life long?

The Shepherds © 2016 John August Swanson | Eyekons

End your family talk with this *collect* for the 3ʳᵈ Sunday of Advent before you *hush* the Advent Candles:
Stir up your power, O Lord, and with great might come among us; and, because we are sorely hindered by our sins, let your bountiful grace and mercy speedily help and deliver us; through Jesus Christ our Lord, to whom, with you and the Holy Spirit, be honor and glory, now and for ever. **Amen.**

....

TUESDAY of this week: Read Isaiah 62:10-12 again and talk about it. Wonder together how it feels to be called "The Holy people of the Lord." What do you think it means to be *holy*?
- When the prophet Isaiah spoke these words, I wonder if the people really listened? I wonder if they could understand? Sometimes the Bible is hard to understand, what are some ways that we might *listen* and understand better?

End your family talk with this ancient advent blessing before you *hush* the Advent Candles: *May the gladness of Christmas, which is HOPE, and the spirit of Christmas, which is PEACE, and the adoration of Christmas, which is JOY, and the heart of Christmas which is LOVE, be ours now and tomorrow and forever.* **Amen.**

Daily Family Readings for this third week of Advent
(you may want to relight your Advent candle each day of the week)

WEDNESDAY of this week: Read Luke 2:25-35. The shepherds were not the only people excited to see baby Jesus! The old man, Simeon, took Jesus in his arms and blessed him! Then he even wrote a song about seeing Jesus (vs. 29-32) and Luke wrote down that song for generations to sing again and again!

Presentation in the Temple © 2016 John August Swanson / Eyekons

- Could you write a song about the baby Jesus?
- What would you want your song to say?

End your family talk with the Song of Simeon before you *hush* the Advent Candles:

Master, dismiss your servant[s] in peace, according to your word; for [our] eyes have seen your salvation, which you prepared in the presence of all people, light for revelation to the Gentiles and for glory to your people Israel.

Color in the 1st – 2nd, and 3rd Advent Candles. Also add the flames.

What color should they be? *(Did you figure out why the 3rd candle is sometimes PINK?)*

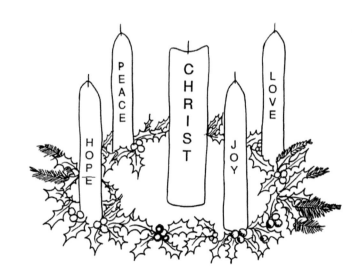

Daily Family Readings for this third week of Advent
(you may want to relight your Advent candle each day of the week)

....

THURSDAY of this week: Read Luke 2:36-38. Not only Simeon was worshiping in the temple day and night at that time, there was also a prophet named Anna. And just like the prophets of old, she *listened* to God. Because she was *listening* to God, she knew right away that the baby was the promised son of God!
- I wonder if the other people in the temple that day *listened* to the good news announced by Simeon and by Anna?
- I wonder what it would be like to see—and recognize—the baby Jesus, and know that he was God's best gift to the world?
- What would you do if you knew this good news to share?

End your family talk with this Swiss blessing (Edelweiss) **before you *hush* the Advent candles:**
May the Lord, mighty God, bless, preserve you and keep you. Give you peace, perfect peace, courage in every endeavor. Life up your eyes and see His face, and His grace forever. May the Lord, mighty God, bless, preserve you and keep you!"

....

FRIDAY of this week: Read the story of the shepherds once more from Luke 2:8-20 and maybe also from *The Jesus Storybook Bible*, pg. 184-191). Can you draw a picture of the shepherds seeing the angels? Or maybe a picture walking toward Bethlehem? Or maybe a picture of them running out to tell the good news to everyone they could find?

End your family talk with a blessing by Timothy Cross before you *hush* the Advent candles: *May the joy of the angels, the eagerness of the shepherds, the perseverance of the wise men, the obedience [and trust] of Joseph and Mary, and the peace of the Christ-child be ours this Christmas; and the blessing of God Almighty, Father, Son, and Holy Spirit, be among us and remain with us always. **Amen.***

Fourth Week of Advent

Epiphany © 2016 John August Swanson | Eyekons

Sometimes we call them "Wise men" and sometimes they are called "Magi"—these visitors from the East are some of the most mysterious characters in the story of Christ's birth! Where did they come from? Why did they come? And for goodness sake, why did they go and ask King Herod where they might find the baby?

We are all on our way to Bethlehem to celebrate the birth of the Christ child (only these wise men arrived a couple of years late!)

The Magi show us the way to Bethlehem by *paying attention & giving our best gifts to the Christ child!*

....

On this 4th Sunday of Advent light _ALL_ the purple (and pink) candles of your Advent wreath!

Fourth Week of Advent - FAMILY call to SABBATH

A Family Call to Sabbath from a parent or other adult:
Joy to the world, the Lord has come!

Family response: *Let earth receive her King!*

....

READ aloud together these scriptures:
(if you have younger children, you may wish to read only the Psalm and Gospel reading. You might also want to read from The Jesus Storybook Bible by Sally Lloyd-Jones, pg. 192-199)

Psalm: Psalm 72:10-14
Old Testament reading: Isaiah 60:1-7
New Testament reading: Luke 1:45-55
Gospel reading: Matthew 2:1-12

....

Fourth Week of Advent - Family Talk-about-It

- Wonder together how the Magi felt when they saw the special star for a king?
- Wonder together how they knew the star was special and others just saw a star?
- Wonder together if it was hard for them to find the special king?
- Wonder together why the Magi brought gifts . . . and wonder what that means for

our own family gift giving and receiving?

Close with a family prayer time—you may say your own and end with the Family Sabbath Prayer and Blessing below….

....

Family Prayer Time *Dear Lord, as we prepare our hearts and our home for your coming this Christmas, help us to be part of your plan to let the whole world know your hope, your peace, your joy and your love. **Amen.***

....

Blessing (before you *hush* your Advent candles) *May the light of Christ come into our home this Christmas season. May the light of Christ lead us to the joy of His Kingdom. Now and forever. Amen.*

....

Advent in the history of the church—DID YOU KNOW?
In the Gospel story the Magi are neither numbered as three nor described as kings (in fact, Matthew is the only gospel writer that even mentions them). In 3rd century the theologian Origen was the first to speak of three; the first time they are called 'kings' is in the 6th century—and they were then given names; in the 8th century it was proposed that the kings represented the three parts of the known world—Asia, Europe and Africa—and came to be depicted racially in art and verse.

Daily Family Readings for this fourth week of Advent

(you may want to relight your Advent candle each day of the week)

MONDAY of this week:

Read Luke 1: 45-55 and talk about Mary's song—talk about what you think it might feel like for your soul to "magnify" the Lord (vs. 46); and what it means to "fear the Lord" (vs. 50); and how God has "brought down the powerful and lifted up the lowly" (vs. 52-53).
- What do you think all this has to do with Christmas?

End your family talk by reading (or singing) words from this Christmas hymn written by Isaac Watts* (1719) before you *hush* **your Advent Candles:** *"Joy to the world! The Lord is come; let earth receive her King; let every heart prepare him room, and heaven and nature sing."*

The Canticle of Zechariah

TUESDAY of this week: Read Luke 1:56-80 and talk about Zechariah's song—

- In what ways do you think God looks favorably on his people? (v 68)
- What do you think it means that God remembered his holy *covenant*? (vs.70-72) (and just what is a *covenant?* Do you know? Can you find out?)
- Did you know that this is the same John (the Baptizer) that baptized Jesus as Jesus began his earthly ministry? (if you want, you can read John's story in Mark 1:1-15 or Luke 3:1-22) *or in The Jesus Storybook Bible,* pg. 200-207*)*

End your family talk by reading (or singing) words from this Christmas hymn written by Isaac Watts* (1719) before you *hush* **your Advent Candles:** *"Joy to the earth! The Savior reigns; let all their songs employ; while fields and floods, rocks, hills, and plains repeat the sounding joy."*

Daily Family Readings for this fourth week of Advent

(you may want to relight your Advent candle each day of the week)

....

WEDNESDAY of this week: Read Luke 2:1-20 and talk again about the night Jesus was born. *You may also want to add the baby Jesus figure to your Manger Scene (Creché) tonight!*

End your family talk by reading (or singing) words from this Christmas hymn written by Isaac Watts* (1719) before you *hush* **your Advent Candles:** *"No more let sins and sorrows grow, nor thorns infest the ground; Christ comes to make his blessings flow far as the curse is found."*

Daily Family Readings for this fourth week of Advent
(you may want to relight your Advent candle each day of the week)

....

THURSDAY of this week: Read aloud some of your families' favorite Christmas books and drink hot cocoa with peppermint sticks and talk about the greatest gift ever given and the greatest gift the world has ever received!

End your family talk by reading (or singing) words from this Christmas hymn written by Isaac Watts* (1719) before you *hush* your Advent Candles: *"He rules the world with truth and grace, and makes the nations prove the glories of his righteousness, and wonders of his love."*

....

FRIDAY of this week: Read aloud some more of your families' favorite Christmas books and talk about what it means for your family to know and love Jesus and be a light in the world to show God's love and hope and peace.

End your family talk by reading (or singing) words from this Christmas hymn written by Isaac Watts* (1719) before you *hush* your Advent Candles: *"Joy to the world! The Lord is come; let earth receive her King; let every heart prepare him room, and heaven and nature sing."*

*Did you know that Isaac Watts wrote nearly 600 hymns and he was called "the father of English hymnody?" (Do you know what a 'hymn' is? You might want to ask your pastor.)

Christmastide

Thus begins the *feast of the Nativity of the Lord!*

After weeks of patient expectation and preparation, now we celebrate with joy and amazement the actual arrival of the "Savior, who is the Messiah, the Lord!"

"The Word became flesh and blood,
  and moved into our neighborhood.
We saw the glory with our own eyes,
  the one-of-a-kind glory,
  like Father, like Son,
Generous inside and out,
  true from start to finish."
                    – John 1, *The Message*

FAMILY call to SABBATH

A Family Call to Sabbath from a grown-up: *Love is like a light shining in a dark place.*

Family response: *As we light these candles we celebrate the love we find in Jesus Christ!*

Presentation in the Temple © 2016 John August Swanson | Eyekons

Week of CHRISTMASTIDE

Re-light the 1st purple candle (for the last time this year)

As you do this, read **Isaiah 52:7-10** and remember that the prophet Isaiah wrote this a long, long time before Jesus was born….how did he know?
- Look at verse 10 again, how will all the *ends of the earth see the salvation of our God?* What does *salvation* mean?

Re-light the 2nd purple candle (for the last time this year)

As you do this, read **Luke 1:45-55** and wonder again how Mary *trusted* God.
- Do you think that Mary was wise?
- What wise things did she say in this passage?
- Wonder together how wisdom and trust go together?

Re-light the 3rd purple (or pink) candle (for the last time this year)

As you do this, read **Hebrews 1:1-6** and wonder again about the joy of the angels and talk about why the Bible tells us that the angels worship God.
Go back and count how many angels are in the painting on the previous page?
- Write the number here _____.
- What else do you see in this painting?

Re-light the 4th purple candle (for the last time this year)

As you do this, read **Micah 5:2** and wonder about how this prophet, who lived at the same time as the prophet Isaiah, also *listened* to God and was able to tell the people that Jesus—the promised Messiah—would be born the little town of Bethlehem—*700 years before Jesus was born!*

Now light your CHRIST CANDLE for the 1st time!

As you do this, read **John 1:1-5 & 9-14** (You might want to read it from *The Message* translation.)
- Wonder together why John starts his Gospel this way.
- Wonder what John means when he calls Jesus Christ *the Word?* - How do you think *the Word* was in the very beginning of time *with God?*

Week of CHRISTMASTIDE - Family Prayer Time

In your prayer today, remember to thank God for the best gift of Jesus Christ! And also thank God for family and gifts and home and …(make your own list of things for which your family is thankful today).

Then you may end with this prayer:
Dear Lord, you are the Word. You are the light of the world. Help us to love your Word and your light and worship you like the angels. **Amen.**

....

Blessing to read (before you *hush* your Advent candles) *May the light of Christ come into our home this Christmastide. May the light of Christ lead us to the joy of His Kingdom. Now and forever.* **Amen.**

....

Christmastide in the history of the church
Commonly called the "Twelve Days of Christmas"—Christmastide is the liturgical church season when we celebrate the birth of Christ. In much of Christian history gifts were given each day of the 12 days of Christmas (instead of all at once on or before Christmas day as we usually do in our American culture.) What might be the advantages of waiting until *after* Advent before giving gifts?

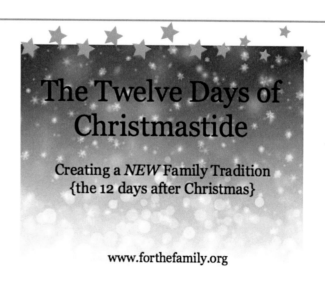

The Twelve Days of Christmastide

Creating a *NEW* Family Tradition
{the 12 days after Christmas}

www.forthefamily.org

Daily Family Readings for the week Christmastide
(you may want to relight your Christ candle each day)

. . . .

MONDAY of this week: *Parents/adults, you may wish to skip over this part if you have younger children. (If you can find a copy of Inos Biffi's illustrated children's book, The Way to Bethlehem, you can read this story on pages 30-31.)*

Right after one of the most joyful days in our church year, December 25 (CHRISTMAS!) comes one of the saddest days, December 28— this is the day the church calls *The Feast of the Holy Innocents* when we remember the time when King Herod did something very sad. You can read about it in Matthew 2:13-23.

Sometimes Churches try to ignore this part of the Christmas story because it is so sad; however, I invite you and your family to wonder together about *why* this story is important and *what* it means for the *HOPE* of Christmas.

- Wonder together why an angel came and warned the holy family to travel to Egypt and not return until after Herod died?
- Wonder together if this story reminds us of the words of the Prophets, that the whole world was in darkness and needed God's gift of the *LIGHT of Christ?*
- I wonder if you and your family can pray for all the children in our world today who also live in darkness and need the light of Christ to shine on them?

End your family talk with this *collect* **for the Holy Innocents before you** *hush* **the Christ Candle:** *We remember today, O God, the slaughter of the holy innocents of Bethlehem by King Herod. Receive, we pray, into the arms of your mercy all innocent victims; and by your great might frustrate the designs of evil tyrants and establish your rule of justice, love, and peace; through Jesus Christ our Lord, who lives and reigns with you, in the unity of the Holy Spirit. One God, forever and ever.* ***Amen***

TUESDAY of this week: Read Matthew 2:14-15 & 19-23.

- Wonder together if God still speaks to people in dreams?
- Do you ever wonder if God desires to speak to us, but our lives are too full of other noises? Maybe in the coming year your family could make a *covenant* (promise) to spend more time with the TV and the music and the cell phones turned off so that you can pay more attention to the things God wants you to know.

End your family talk with this blessing of St. Patrick before you *hush* the Christ Candle: *May the strength of God pilot us; may the wisdom of God instruct us; May the hand of God protect us; may the word of God direct us; be always ours this day and forever more.* **Amen.**

WEDNESDAY of this week: Read Luke 2: 33-52.

- Wonder together about why Jesus—at age 12—astonished and amazed his parents and the religious leaders.
- Ask your parents/grandparents how they'd feel if you just disappeared without letting them know!
- Do you think Mary and Joseph were upset?
- What does verse 51 say Jesus did after returning home to Nazareth?
- Wonder together what verse 52 tells us about Jesus?

End your family talk with this *collect* for the second Sunday after Christmas before you *hush* the Christ Candle: *God who comes now to us with the power of your Holy Spirit, call us who are made in your image always to love what is most deeply human, as you do, so that human beings everywhere might know how much they are loved and valued. We pray in the power of your incarnation.* **Amen.**

Daily Family Readings for the week Christmastide
(you may want to relight your Christ candle each day)

. . . .

THURSDAY of this week: Read Isaiah 9:6-7. Talk about the names for Jesus Christ in verse 6, how many different names are listed here?
- Wonder together how they all describe Jesus. Grown-ups, help your children think about and begin to understand all that these names mean.

End your family talk with this *collect* for Epiphany before you *hush* the Christ Candle: *We are star-struck, radiant God, by your glory and graciousness to us: Shine your light through us that we may point all peoples to your ways through our living. In the Holy Name of Jesus, we pray. **Amen.***

. . . .

FRIDAY of this week: Read Philippians 2:5-18 and talk together about beginning a new year as a family ready to *shine God's light and love* in the world! Verse 12 says to *work out your salvation with fear and trembling*—wow!
- What do you think *that* means? The word *fear* doesn't always mean *being afraid.*
- Wonder together what else it means to *fear* something or someone?
- Can you find out and talk about it?

End your family talk with a blessing from Philippians 4:7 before you *hush* the Christ Candle: *May the peace of God, that transcends all human understanding, guard your hearts and your minds in Christ Jesus.*

Presentation in the Temple © 2016 John August Swanson | Eyekons

Epiphany

The Wise men made a careful, costly, and lengthy search to find the new born King and found him in an unlikely place. I wonder if like those Magi of long ago, an important part of your family's growing faith might involve seeking and searching for the Lord in unlikely places this year!

An important point of our celebration of **Epiphany** is shining the light of God's word in unlikely places...seeking and searching to find God where you least expect to while getting to know God better! *And so - even today - wise men (and wise women....and wise children) are still seeking & finding our way to Bethlehem!*

....

One delightful way to celebrate **Epiphany** is to prepare and eat a **Three Kings' Cake** with friends and family. In this symbolic search for the baby Jesus, children and adults gather to eat a delicious cake with a toy baby hidden inside.

"Three King's Cake" created by Emily Okholm Ganzer

The person who finds the baby hidden in their piece of cake gets to tell again the story of the Magi's search…
then the whole family can talk about ways that your faith involves seeking & searching the Lord in unlikely places!

(For recipes and ideas check online)

Week of EPIPHANY - FAMILY call to SABBATH

Light your family's CHRIST CANDLE as a way to prepare for Sabbath keeping.

A Family Call to Sabbath from a grown-up: The Word of the Lord *came*....

Family response: hope for all people cradled in his arms.

Grown-up: The Word if the Lord *comes*....

Family response: calling us out or our comfort zones, to go where grace is needed most.

Grown-up: The Word if the Lord *will* come....

Family response: gathering all the outsiders & insiders into one big family of God!

. . . .

READ aloud together: *(if you have younger children, you may wish to read only the Old & New Testament readings.)*

Psalm: 119:97-109
Old Testament reading: Isaiah 60:1-6
New Testament reading: 1 John 1:5-9
Gospel reading: John 8:12-19

Epiphany in the history of the church—DID YOU KNOW?

The word "epiphany" means "manifestation" (Having an *epiphany* is like having an *AH-HA!* moment when the light goes on and we begin to see things more clearly.) Traditionally, Epiphany is celebrated on January 6 (at the end of the 12 Days of Christmastide). Often an Epiphany feast completes the season of Christmas by inviting us to figure out the identity of the Christ child.

Three traditions—baking a *Three King's Cake*, marking a door lintel with the *Magi's Blessing*, and filling the churches worship space with *lighted candles*— all help us move from the season with more faith-forming experiences and memories than simply following our cultural cues!

Week of EPIPHANY - Family Talk-about-it

- Wonder together why the Bible talks so much about *light*—why is light important? What is light for?
- When do you most need light?
- What happens when there is no light?
- Can you imagine being in a place where no light shines at all?

Close with a family prayer time—you may say your own and end with the Family Sabbath Prayer and Blessing:

Family Prayer Time *Dear Lord, Your light has come, but sometimes we seem to prefer the darkness of temptation & desire. Lord, we confess our sins to You and pray that your light will shine in all the dark corners of our lives.* **Amen.**

Blessing to read (before you *hush* your Christ candle)
May the light of Christ come into our home this Epiphany season. May the light of Christ lead us to the joy of His Kingdom. Now and forever. **Amen.**

Daily Family Readings for the week of Epiphany
(you may want to relight your Christ candle each day)

....

MONDAY of this week: Read Matthew 4:16-25. Think of all the ways that Jesus began to shine *light* in the world!
- How many ways can you find in Matthew 4:16-25?

Before you *hush* the Christ Candle today, end your family talk by *writing* the traditional *Magi Blessing* **on the lintel of your door.**

You might want to use oil or you can use a piece of chalk to mark a cross over the main door your family uses to come and go each day. As you mark the door lintel, say this blessing:

Peace to this house and to all who dwell within; peace and joy to guests who enter here; lead us not into temptation, but deliver us from evil and may our hearts and minds reflect your light in our neighborhood and in our world. **Amen.**

(Also, you may want to write "20+C+M+B+19" over or beside your door! Read about it below.)

....

TUESDAY of this week: Read Matthew 5:1-20.
- How many times does Jesus use the word *blessed?*
- Wonder together what it means to be blessed.
- Wonder what it means for you to be like *salt & light.*
- Look at verse 16, and write down 5 ways that your family can be God's *light* this year.
(You may want to post this list somewhere visible in your home!)

End your family talk with this blessing of St. Patrick before you *hush* the Christ Candle: *May the strength of God pilot us; may the wisdom of God instruct us; May the hand of God protect us; may the word of God direct us. Be always ours this day and forever more.* **Amen.**

Daily Family Readings for the week of Epiphany
(you may want to relight your Christ candle each day)

....

WEDNESDAY of this week: Read John 8:12 and be reminded again of the light that Jesus Christ brought into the whole world. A Germany custom is to hold a *Children's Three King's Day Festival* between January 1 & 6. After

worship at church the children dress up as kings and go from house to house gathering offerings for poor children in poor countries. They carry sticks with stars on the top. At the homes they sing songs and paint (or chalk?) the letters **"20+C+M+B+19"** for the Latin

Christus Mansionem Benedicat
(Christ bless this house + the current year).

End your family talk with this traditional German blessing before you *hush* the Christ Candle: *With faith there is love, with love there is peace, with peace there is blessing, with blessing, there is God, with God there is no need.* **Amen.**

....

THURSDAY of this week: Read Psalm 27:1.
- Wonder together why it is easy to be afraid and sometimes so hard to trust.
- How is the Lord our God both our *light* and our *salvation?*
- What do *you* think *salvation* mean?

End your family talk with this family blessing before you *hush* the Christ Candle: *May God bless our family. May God strengthen each one under this roof. May God dwell in our hearts. May God inspire us to share God's love with one another. And may we always know that we are held in God's arms of love.*

Daily Family Readings for the week of Epiphany

(you may want to relight your Christ candle each day)

FRIDAY of this week: Read Luke 11:33-36.

- How do you think you can keep your "eyes healthy" and your "whole body full of light?"

End your family talk with this *collect* **for Epiphany before you** *hush* **the Christ Candle:** *We are star-struck, radiant God, by your glory and graciousness to us: Shine your light through us that we may point all peoples to your ways through our living. In the Holy Name of Jesus, we pray.* **Amen.**

Challenge your parents (or other adults) to discover how many Bible stories you can find in the candle picture above that tell us about Epiphany! (*EPIPHANY = the light of Christ coming into our world.*)

Made in the USA
San Bernardino, CA
23 October 2018